C L A U S !

ALSO BY MICHAEL C. WITTE

The Book of Terns (with Peter Delacorte)

AS ILLUSTRATOR

Tenderfeet and Ladyfingers, by Susan Kelz Sperling

An Owl Book

HOLT, RINEHART AND WINSTON

NEW YORK

To Mom, Dad, and Marcia for Christmas past.
To Sally, Griff, Spence, and Jasper
for Christmas present and future.

Published by Holt, Rinehart, and Winston, 383 Madison Avenue, New York, New York 10017.
Published simultaneously in Canada by Holt, Rinehart and Winston of Canada, Limited.

Library of Congress Catalog Card Number: 82-82710
ISBN 0-03-061749-9

First Edition

Printed in the United States of America
1 3 5 7 9 10 8 6 4 2

THE CLAUS OF IT ALL

A CLAUS APPROXIMATION

A NEEDY CLAUS

DEPENDENT CLAUS

INDEPENDENT CLAUS

CLAUS TO THE VEST

A CLAUS FOR CELEBRATION

DANCING CLAUS

A CLAUS ACQUAINTANCE

CLAUS TO CAPACITY

GETTING CLAUS TO HOME

ESCAPE CLAUS

A TOUCH OF CLAUS

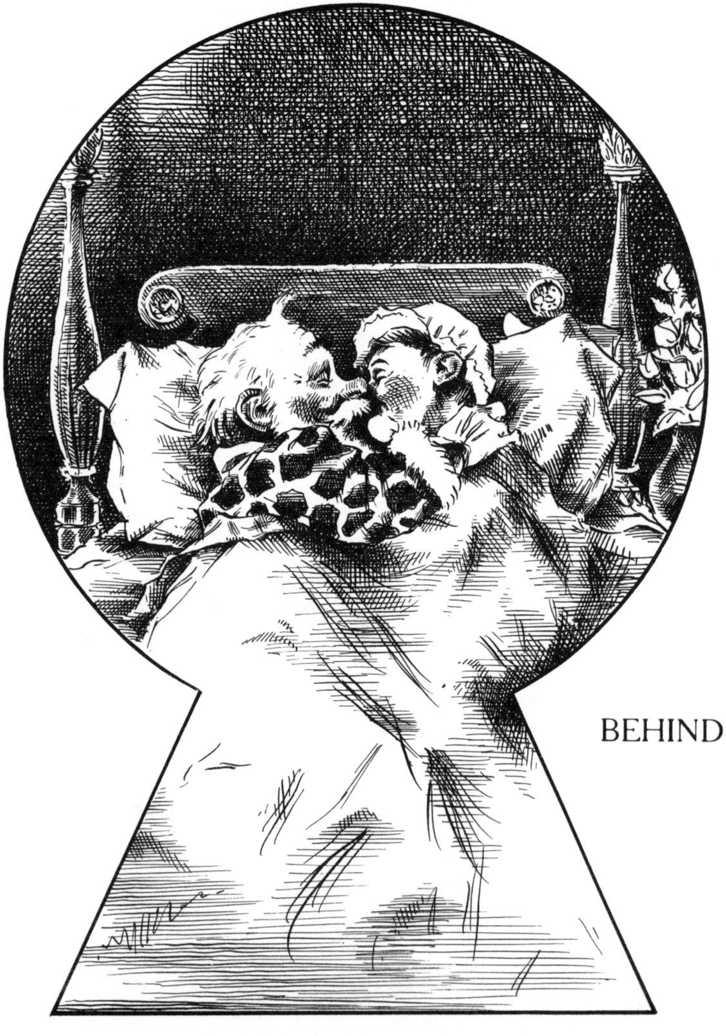

BEHIND CLAUS DOORS

RULING CLAUS

CLAUS STRUGGLE

IN CLAUS ACCORD

CLAUS ASSOCIATES

SINGING IN CLAUS HARMONY

KEEPING CLAUS TRACK

A CLAUS LIKENESS

CLAUS-CÉLÈBRE

Why me?

A CLAUS INSPECTION

HAMMER CLAUS

CLAUS CONTACT

CAT CLAUS

COOKING CLAUS

CLAUS TO THE BONE

THE CLAUS OF INFLATION

TOO CLAUS FOR COMFORT

EXERCISE CLAUS

CLAUS BUT NO CIGAR

CLAUS TO THE DEADLINE

A CLAUS ADVISER

GRANDFATHER CLAUS

BARE CLAUS

A CLAUS SHAVE

A CLAUS-ACTION SUIT

WORKING IN CLAUS COORDINATION

CLAUS TO LIFTOFF

CLAUS FRIENDS AND RELATIONS

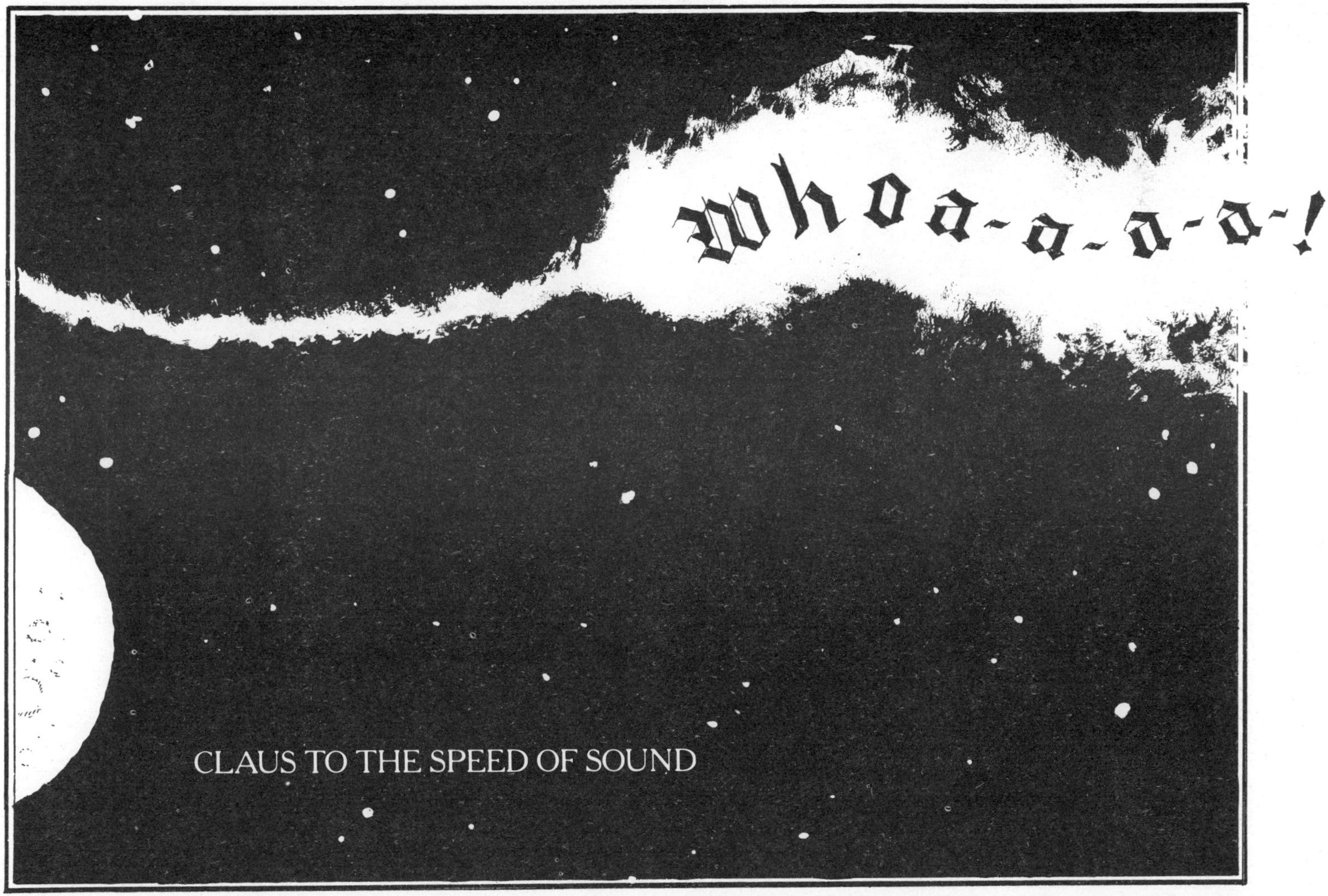
Whoa-a-a-a-!
CLAUS TO THE SPEED OF SOUND

LOST CLAUS

CLAUS TO A BREAKTHROUGH

CLAUS TO DISASTER

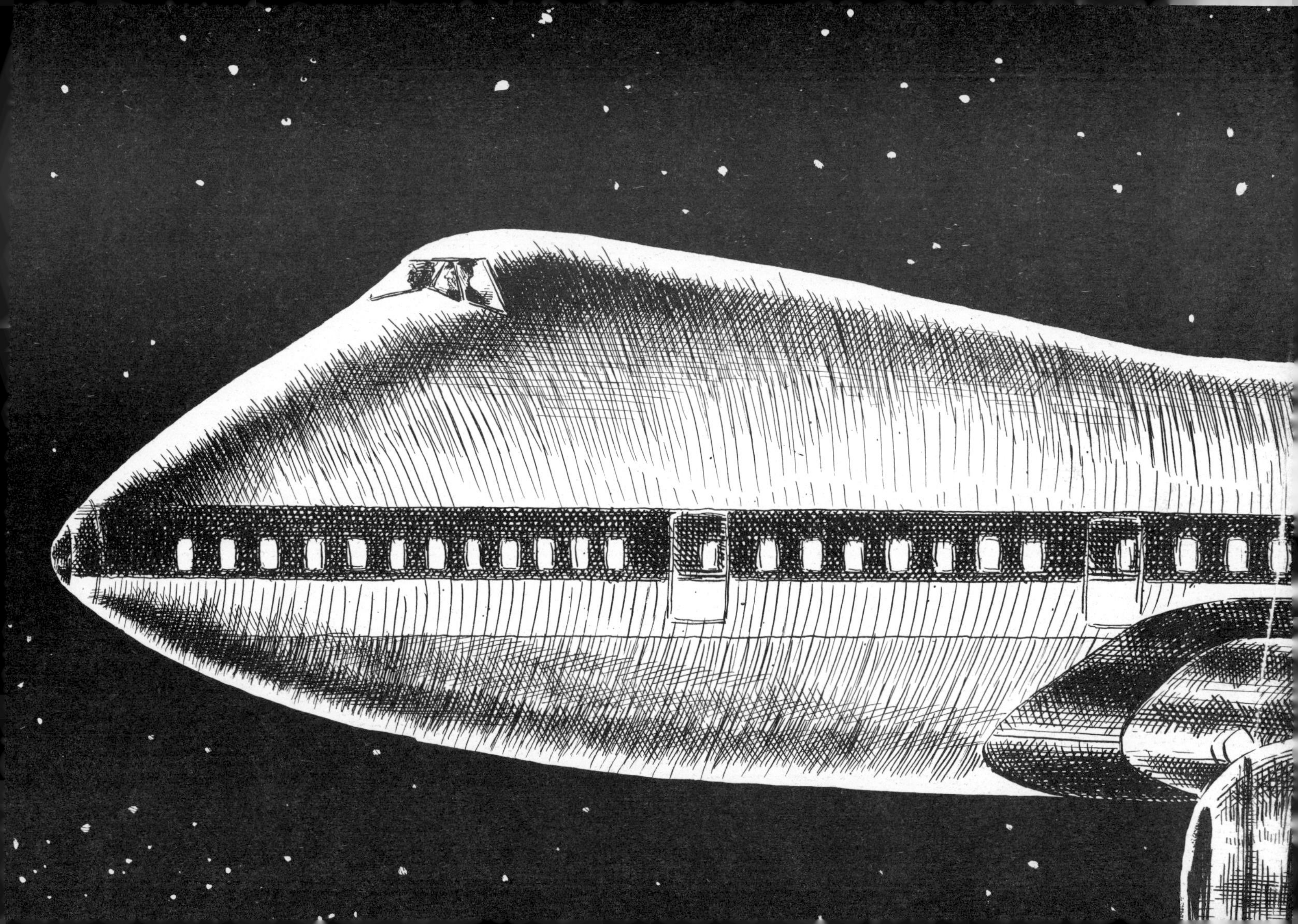

NO CLAUS FOR ALARM

A CLAUS FIT

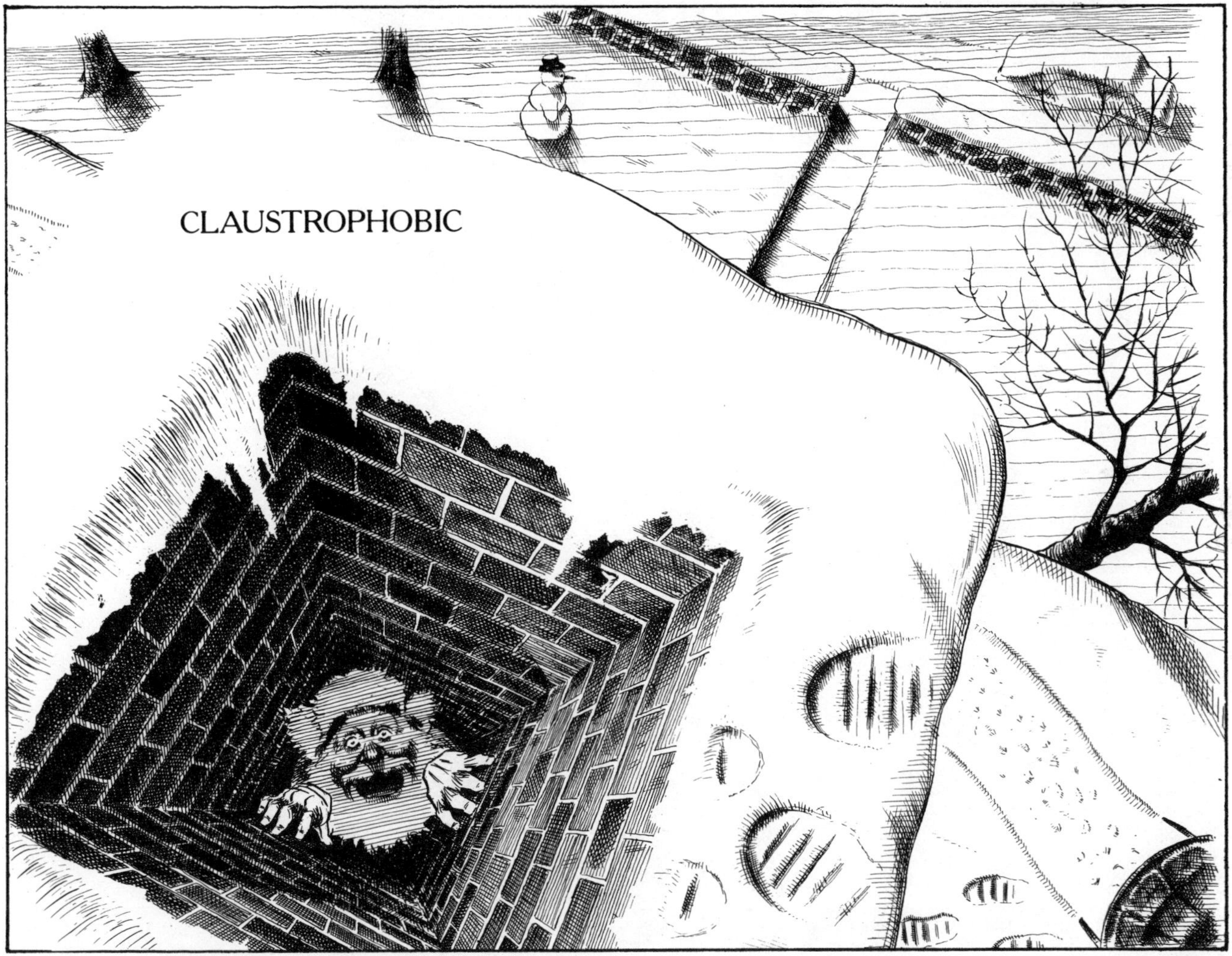
CLAUSTROPHOBIC

CLAUS QUESTIONING

SACK, CLAUS AND ASHES

CLAUS OBSERVERS

A CLAUS ENCOUNTER

CLAUS TO TEARS